THE
QUIET

THE FILTHY QUIET

Kate Noakes

Parthian, Cardigan SA43 1ED www.parthianbooks.com
First published in 2019
© Kate Noakes 2019
ISBN 978-1-912681-02-0
Editor: Susie Wild
Cover design by Alison Evans
Typeset by Elaine Sharples
Printed and bound by 4edge Limited, UK
Published with the financial support of the Welsh Books Council British
Library Cataloguing in Publication Data
A cataloguing record for this book is available from the British Library.

For Charlotte and Angharad, my lovely girls, always.

Contents

The threshold

Doormats are by-products
copra, coconut husks dried
shredded, tough enough
for decades of trodden-in mud.

> *I am flesh, bone, blood, nerve.*

Picture: me on a mound of coconuts
the processing plant, Tonga, '69
wearing a navy dress
with red frills at collar, sleeve, skirt edge.

> *I am flesh, bone, blood, nerve.*

My hair is pixie-short. Close in
where I wiped my hand on my cheek
there's milk from the macheted coconut
I drank that morning.

> *I am practising, blood, nerve.*

Swans have no need of necklaces

As if swirled in a river bed
I watch the clatter of stones
their desire to break free
from my neck and tumble
home via paving slabs and cobbles.

I follow the flow of silver from my throat
into gratings and drains
dabble at this latest scattering.

Pen-me snatches feed, wonders what
will happen with malachite
after labradorite I lost my job
post-pearl, my love, and tonight
in an ebonied sky, the moon hangs full.

Three Things about Mick

I – Wardrobes and other potential disasters

Mick liked holes in his clothes. *I look cool*, he told himself, *hobo style*, but really he was too indolent to either take to the road, or thread a needle. Like showers, washing machines frightened him, though once a month he was compelled to visit the launderette. All the neighbourhood girls, and women who remembered with fondness a particular Levi's commercial, circled that day on their calendars. They let their machines flood, so they had to go for a service wash. Though he didn't know it, Mick was a very well put together, good looking boy.

II – Needing a punchbag

Mick often woke filled with an anger for which he had no explanation, or none he wanted to share with anyone, had there been anyone there. He looked around for a cat, knowing all he'd ever spent his life with had left with their mistresses. Mick had taken to attacking the furniture, but scratched bed posts and chests of drawers were much less pliable than feline flesh and fur. He knew that, and could easily have reminded himself of the fact had he looked at his purpled toes before launching the next assault on an inanimate object. One day it was the fridge, which, being modern, yielded to his double flying kick. There are now two odd-shaped footprints in the thin steel door. Mick, nursing a broken collarbone from where he landed awkwardly, is yet more angry.

III – Red star in the morning

Mick said everything he did was work, from cleaning his teeth to picking the fluff from his navel, which he didn't do too often. There was a lot of effort involved in simply being, especially as he lived mainly on whiskey. After a while Mick began to shrink. His keen musculature melted into malted flesh. His skin paled and needed colouring with caramel, his little secret. His mind began to mash up memories. The angels were taking their share. He said his name to the mirror. No one replied *Hello, Mick*.

I pack you in my bags by mistake

The mountains I must cross before I reach
the sea are made of all ages of rock.

I can see you in the dip in their spine
the place in my back where you rest your hand.
You're there all right beyond the cotton grass
flax, red heather and new-bald summer sheep.

Under the grey stone walls tumbling down
deep in rot and root reach, thick in the peat
beneath the feet of angry cattle and ravens
with myths of big cats, is where your heart lies.

Night, when the ruthless wind stunts the hawthorn
I can hear you roaring the sodden earth
your voice rocking the bog. Banshee. Demon.

The sun makes me

want to head north
flee the jobs that need doing
seek retreat
in the land of midnight

and wish for repose
in the hut of six aspens
leaves silvering the breeze
under its roof of
moss and saxifrage
flecked blue by harebells
on implausible stems

and wish for wood smoke
wild thyme to scent
my thin shirt in a shiver
as I cradle a mug of tea
and look for coming night
its charged promises
its dance of light

and wish to leave the ladder
unpainted, just two rungs
stained as green
as the short-lived grass
where it hides its feet.

Certainly, you are not from Ireland

Clarion clear
   I heard it at the start
      the tap of heel on stone
         with each step
            but it's hip click
            the catch of vertebrae
         twisting sinuous
      side-winding
through damp streets
   rattle, rattle, rattle.
      I should've heeded
         your faint lisp
            the tuning of tongue
            against sharp teeth
         but I trusted
      and lost sight of signs
your bite, a scratch
   that swelling
      and head heat
         nothing wrong.
            Too late, too late
         I've let my blood
      flow from me
   for months, years
as if I could spare it
   and your eyes
      give nothing
         from their black pits.

Glass

I

It's not a looking glass, except as means
of measuring you. *Cheers*, you say raising
a toast, eyes avoiding mine.
Chin, Chin, I reply.

II

It's the chipped windscreen and you cursing
the power of the road, though insured
and replaceable, unlike that born of heat,
the controlled breath of a bare-armed man.

III

It's bowl clear for the colour of wine,
its stem a twist of water and weed.
Pity the chip against the tap
your careless washing up.

IV

Shoreside, I fill a jar with opaque treasure
Roman? Venetian? more likely the smash
of a bottle by a kid like you
too scared to douse a beach fire.

There is only this

Lightning forks, strikes close
no second interval
thunder cracks overhead.
The cream stone I lean on
is warm. The rain is fat
forceful. Step in a pool
you're entering a bath.

Three half-naked boys slip-slide
down the Paseo di Marti
laugh and scream
to the sea. I give chase
can't catch them as they cross
the brilliance between
one darkness and the next.
Things not meant to be. This.

Line-dancing at lunchtime

Today I chose Texas
and friends who don't touch
not that I can smell the smudge
of sage brush or feel
yellow-rose-heat
in this marble-halled mall.

I'm tired of diminutive
Argentines handling me
around the floor, poppet
and like a true star
I'd rather do this alone
one foot-tap-turn at a time.

Pity of it is the neck
of the man in front
pulsating with acne
a galaxy boils furious
between checked collar
and oiled hairline.

For a while I feast on its carrion
stretch my dormant wings, fly.

Intifada, or the crow's carol

Crows carol the valley
an aubade
over a remnant fire.

Shepherds and flocks
have long moved
from the hill.

There is gold grass
to caw
and fight about.

Between black rocks
oily with dawn
an early lamb

bloodied with afterbirth
yellow cord
froth mouth, dried.

Cry that
to whomever will listen
succour, support.

IM Red Rag

Long ago, my once beloved, in the days when posting gig-flyers
for anarcho-punk bands on a carefully routed 3am circuit of town
was radical, mixing wallpaper paste an art, and the streets un-
filmed and quiet, except for cats, the most useful piece of data
was the weekly list of number plates of unmarked police cars, but
this was before you could carry enough computing power in your
pocket for a small city, so I'm not sure how we were meant to
memorise them, or what to do if we actually saw one – a Balaclava
moment perhaps, or time to turn tail, and run.

Ossicles, Ossuary

The tickle has turned into an itch
red-faced and steaming

still secret, but unscratchable
though I try to reach eczema

impossibly in the canal of my left ear
with something smaller than my elbow

as your rage bangs malleus against incus
incus against stapes, stapes against drum

hums a threat: the cat's in the room
you're locking the door.

The proof of being able to cook

It's happening again.
I can feel fat
settling around
my hips, adipose
in my bones
my scars stretching.

I don't want it to set up home.
It's as welcome
as a cat-left frog
that thrashes and gulps
on the doormat,
skin unable
to breathe,
ripped body spilling

guts into the pile
a bilious experiment
in electricity.

The curse of Minerva

is not
that she's
like
Cassandra

no

she's believed
right enough

just not
liked
for being
clever

must be
the owl
thing

huge eyes
long manicure

her
penchant
for the dark

but more

the lack
of mercy
she shows
to mice

chases away
most men.

Are there any women here?

for all rape victims executed under perversions of Sharia law

The kindness is we let you choose
your own stone. We recommend granite
for its triple-minerals, weight
and strength born of fire.
We've come pre-armed, but, over to you
he said, convinced by his fist-long beard
he was being true.

When wrist-bound, he threw me
on my back in the pick-up and drove
the edge of the field. He was smiling
under and over his beard, smiling
as dust rose from the bare football pitch
as the shaft was dug in rainless dirt, smiling
as I was lowered by my feet
as my vertical grave was filled to my neck
as the first rough-cut rock struck my temple
and the next and the next
smiling, smiling
as blood closed my eyes
smiling
as my head filled with quartz.

Stitching the rose

You tie one rose, two, but there's more
take a pruning knife, secateurs
sharp, quick, you nip each bud.
There'll be no celebrations, love.

Felicia, Damask, Floribunda, Blaze

You wield a curved needle
a scimitar of false gut glints
stitches melt into her petals
knot velvet in a fixed embrace.

Elina, Isphahan, Escapade, Grace

Fear does not care much: hybrid tea
rambler, miniature, always these –
embroidery obsessed by blood
though you won't dethorn every shrub.

Medea

I

Be my gold bird, not cowardly cock crowing
come morning, or finch flocking the sunflowers.

They won't do for you to mirror sea and sky
rather be a bird that can really fly

and more than fly, mountain soar
upland ewes in your claws.

I want you as eagle, hook-billed and able to spin flesh
into a golden feast for our sons in their lamb-lined nest.

*

I've studied rank hedgerow herbs all my life
can tincture purple-hooded aconite

distil dark yew, foxglove and baneberry
drip poison from hemlock and bryony

boil white hellebore with laburnum seed
add deadly nightshade and calabar bean.

Love, I'm the one to help you now
take me here for wife and I'll show you how.

*

Look well at the khalkotauroi and look again
if you think there's anything simple about oxen.

This task is hard. Look at their hooves again
shod with an alloy of copper and tin

bronze swords downtrodden, no ordinary herd.
They'll crush and sling you if you're not prepared.

Aeetes meant more when he said flame
than the reddled tan of their hides. Look again.

Their breath smokes the air, none without fire
the blaze is Helios-hot and higher

fiercer than you can stand.
To yoke beasts to your command

will take more than a brave stomach and spleen
you'll need to be fireproof, sun-screened

but as I've studied rank herbs all my life
rest happy with your clever wife

and take this ointment to anoint your skin
cover yourself in unguent as plough day begins.

It will protect you and quickly the four-acre field
will be scratched, crooked, tilled.

*

Stop now my love, come home
let me bathe your ache-sore bones

it's time for wine from the cask
and to rest well for tomorrow's task.

*

Broadcast your strength, scatter seed
today is for bragging your deeds.

From this soft leather pouch you'll prise
inch-long points of bloodied enamel, flesh dried

at their fire-formed roots: dragon's teeth remain
tougher than the hard-paste porcelain.

There'll be no surprise as the strange harvest
of living skin springs from its earthy rest.

You'll remember what to do
be like Cadmus, find your glittering jewel.

Black basalt will be your igneous ally
you'll cast it into the ranks till they fly

confused, and unable to tell friend from foe
will kill one another, and so it goes.

*

Walk away love, come home
leave crows to pick bones

more wine from the cask
rest before your last task.

*

The fleece hangs in a salt-bleached tree
precious-spun as your feather hair and so downy

it drips riches like rain into veins of rock
no need to swoop streams clawing for luck.

All that glisters here is gold
yours for taking, mine to hold.

One more challenge, the sleepless dragon
but I've a solution for her you can count on

I've studied rank herbs and extracted a fix
of castor beans, pressed into an oily mix.

Fool her with flattery, the whitening of her eyes
and ricin lotion artfully disguised

will keep her youthful, the new royal jelly
she won't feel the burn in her throat or belly.

*

Take your prize love, you're done
it's time for Pelias to give up his throne.

II

Practising persuasion, not a new feat
important if the old man decides to cheat

fails on his promises, changes his mind
tricks us with memory, fleeces us blind.

My victim, the monster, Talos of Crete
is huge and trusting, easy to defeat.

See how simply he'll give up his life.
Yes, I am your clever wife.

The bronze nail keeping his one vein locked
is as loose as the lid on Pandora's box.

Long life, my ruby eyes and silvery tongue
will quick work their magic, his blood'll be gone.

*

Don't be shocked love, it's nothing new, a mere
sharpening of the skills we may need when we're there.

*

Untrue to his word, the lying old goat
has stashed the fleece, now I'll slash his throat.

His daughters love and cherish that old bore
they'll wish they didn't with what I have in store.

What every man desires is youth
and I can grant him this – the truth

is that is pliable, can be bent
and they'll trust me, love, when they shouldn't.

I'll use my cauldron, in it I'll cram
a quickly slaughtered, quartered ram

and by a trick from your clever wife
a fresh lamb will gambol into life.

They'll believe the evidence of their eyes
you and I know is nothing but lies;

from girls' hands to pot the old man's guts will flow
fast dead he'll be, and so it goes.

*

Love, there's nothing so very amazing in this
you're now a king, wasn't that your wish?

So why all the talk of canals and Cornith?
Rest here, at least for the wine months.

III

I saw your glinting look, before I heard
you were no longer my golden bird

my fierce-clawed eagle of mountain and sea
but lover to Creon's daughter, Glauce.

Marry her then, you'll make a handsome pair
there are plenty more raptors in the air

your sons you'll be leaving all the same
don't hunt the hills for us again.

Memeros and Pheres'll be mine, all mine
sling your hook-bill, spin another your lines.

*

I've studied rank herbs all my life
see how cleverly I'll despatch this new wife

many a root I can grind to powder
to fool her with the perfume of flowers

and soak her wedding gown in poisonous scent
which she'll take for a present that bastard has sent.

It'll work dark acid magic on her happiest day
char her fair skin and slim bones clean away

and as for Creon, as help her he does
he'll burn like his precious one, and so it goes.

*

What love, no surprise, no toasting in wine
no heaping of praise on your clever wife this time?

Cask sorrows, come home, home to me
like the sailor you are, home from the sea.

No? Mourn then as if your heart is broken in two
it sickens me how we're finally through.

Soar out of my sight, my golden bird
don't forget the fleece or these parting words

I'll make you watch your clever wife
a knife to our gold chicks, stopping their lives.

See how I'll slice their sweet necks at the vein
I'll wait till they're sleeping, they won't wake again.

These are my most solemn vows
no boys to succeed you, and so it goes.

You don't think I'll go through with it, I haven't
the strength. You've forgotten the hours I've spent

studying rank herbs and the thousands of ways
to conjure death with a phrase.

I'll do it though it will wrench me to the core.
Watch where you sleep when you're next onshore.

Salomé in the mirror

I find myself calling for your head
on a brass platter from Bernese
the kind I can make into a table

I smile
I smile
manic   delighted

There will be no church
or mosaic shrine
on the spot where this happens

I smile
I smile
manic   delighted

I'll take just your cheek   slashed
The slip of your occasional razor
will do it   for now

I smile
I smile
manic   delighted

You are no saint
and my veils are not translucent.
I can't dance that way anymore.

Penelope: identity theft

I chose the hardest fibres
to strip my skin
jute, copra

to slice the whorls
from my fingertips
hessian, raw flax.

I am weaving lead.

Forth, back
the shuttle flies
the cloth wefted red.

Right, left
the peddles tread
my legs, my legs.

Sundown, yards done
well, not yet.
I sink on my bed
my head, my head.

The clamour from
the waiting boys too much
'Wed me.' 'No, me instead.'

In darkest night
I cut the warp and pull
unthread, unthread.

My new skin
pricks with dread.

Crime of passion domestic violence counting

1. I'm shallow-breathed, flat under the table and

2. aching everywhere, as a blood tear meanders into my hair and

3. sink-holes in my ear, stopping the echo and

4. I fix on the rough planks, biroed and

5. crayoned by one of the girls, I know not which, and

6. this from years ago, I've not seen before and

7. I wonder when, or why, and

8. what was I doing, or where I was at the time, and

9. the stick figure mother smiles green, flashes red teeth and

10. waves her long purple hands, and

From the tower, the sea

All day I gnaw chicken bones and pace
bare boards as splinters pierce my soles.

I wait for the sun to fall fast, to flame; a ball tossed
and twirled in the streets of my childhood
on New Year's Eve and me, eager girl, smiling
against the black for a promise.

Dark comes. The sea inks itself before my tower,
sparks with a million creatures. Rescue seems
possible with these stars glowing in the surf.

Night on night I think to fashion them
into a rope, believe I can knot luminescence
and climb myself free, but there's no shining armour
to bind cold light in this indigo

so I sleep on the bony chair and weep
wooden tears when too soon it is dawn.

The filthy quiet

I – Panorama

My eye is on the mountain in late
afternoon light, its monastery alive
the darkness of pines I can smell
from here, the rocky island
silhouetted in the bay

and you
in blueness, the soft sky

sea and the shops
selling Napoli shirts
but it has to be these
small plum tomatoes grown
on the slopes of Vesuvius
so sweet, so special.

II – Pompeii

Arms thrown back, face down
dirt-wards, I mistake plaster bodies
for inescapable ash
a set too hard to take in

and you
saying I've smothered, drained you

it's easier for passengers to sit
on the train than take the wheel

skimming the hem of the volcano.
I would've handed it to you had there been
a direction worth following.

III – Herculaneum

Lava, tufa, cinder, rock
for an easy build, hands
unburdened by pumice, add brick
tile and there we have it, a town
with marble for altars, few columns
buildings in the shadow
of a smouldering peak.
Make your house on a bulge
in the mantle and expect burning

and you
blowing the top from the cauldron

and I am no longer a complacent
citizen dailying about my life.
You say, even now, you want me
home, sealed in ashes
or facing another fire?

IV – Nel mercato

Melon-sized lemons, thick-rinded,
ripening, hang heavy
in solo nets, plucked from trees
without tearing branches

and you and me
on different stalls either side of the sea

deciding how this will work.
I hope for enough sugar and skill
to spit pips without taking out an eye
or burning my stomach anymore.
Already drops of bile feed back
I've not brought any kaolin or morph.

V – Negozi chiesa

Monstrances, incense, statues,
robes, religious bling, how many
precious Jesuses need cribs?

and you
pretending it's my fault

leaving you standing, naked
in the light as a babe, unable to fend
for yourself. What stopped you?
You are not a child.

VI – Sotto la villa color ocra

A white bearded goat nibbles
shoots on the cliff
sure-footed me on the right
though stony path

and you
busy excavating, rerouting

making forks appear, switching back
forth, confused. The road is through
wild rosemary, self-seeded mustard
heat rising from the tarmac
a beacon, flaming.

VII – Il parco giochi

Wisteria purples the air sweet
for a moment of childishness.
I swing under its scent, you
beside me, our legs
too long for the ground
my seat squeaking

and yours
silent as spring

as the gap growing between us
small as the leap to earth
when much can happen
in those seconds of flight
before the drop.

VIII – Capodimonte

The art collection in its decrepit
palazzo of ox blood walls is

impossible, even down to its café
serving soggy pizza.
We walk miles for a Caravaggio
Christ flayed

and you
emptying my heart

leave tatters, close down sections
of my past, declare them over
blacked out, filled with chairs
where I am no longer allowed to sit.

IX – Palazzo Reale

Sumptuous in its gold, its swags
clocks and ornaments pushed
to the sides of the splendid rooms
floors sheened high, but closely
in the royal palace there's
dust, the dirt of decades

and you
leaving us.

The turtle's back is broken

Give your knuckles some blood
exhale, exhale, exhale

now that you have let go
the world it held changes

gravel shifts by the idle rake
wisteria whips as it pleases

moss runs over the basin
acers spread finger shade

water buffalo, unyoked, forage
in the lakes of their choosing.

The mountain has moved.

In sheds and other refuges

The back of the cave
where stone drips incessantly
is the place men go to think
about what, I don't know.

Later, could be days, weeks, months
even, in extremis, years
they emerge blinking
silent or perhaps softly muttering.

Later still, there may be a story
an apology, an explanation
usually nothing you were thinking
but, at least, something.

Back in the cave, the fire
needs tending, the pots stirring
kids grow in a blink
and the truth finds its grave.

Turning over, Daphne

I was paper
thin skinned
flaking

an avocado stone
set plump on a tripod
over a water dish

soaking
my wax body
till I cracked

split to my fat neck
as if liquid
would be the death of me.

Three sticks arrowed my flesh
so deeply
might have been a thousand

and yet
a root began, translucent
tentatived into fluid

stretched, branched
strengthened
boldened

from my head, a cotyledon
a pair of young leaves
a stem, more.

Consider why we end up

at the table by the door as the wind
sweeps down littered streets
stirs, skitters, scatters
cold debris behind it
hollow pizza boxes, screwed up cups
spent sugar papers, and blasts in
over our food freezing it, and
our conversation with each
new entrant to this final scene.

Fitting, as we are putting
everything on deep ice, and
we both know there'll be
no thaw, surely, no spring.

Reading, the town I never wanted

I will soon forget the green of goose shit
on the river bank, the viciousness of swans
the lion's misplaced feet, walls not let down

where two or is it three rivers run
the old name of the pub, you know that one
that the Dole is an arts centre, the Post a wine bar
the cut across campus isn't too far.

I need to lose the memory of brick and flint
pea shingle, drowned dumps and gravel pits
the Whitley whiff, January's floodplain lakes
chalk bomb craters, lime kilns, museum fakes.

I shall not recall the way from Earley
to the cemetery, which junction is best
to take me to Woodley or Reading West.

No tears to see the back of Caversham
precinct, Terry's pound shop, the kebab van.

I won't remember the price of the train
the bus number, your name, your bloody name.
Yes, it's mostly this I'll wipe from my brain.

Elements for benign banishment

O northern earth, hold her from sinking
in his soft clay, make loess fruitless
to her touch, fold her back to sand
to heat, your gentle metamorphosis.

      Cayenne pepper and white sage anti-clockwise

Soft, O water of the west, launch her safe
and clear from silted rivers, float her free
from the man with canals in his heart,
settle her in small ponds, your safe mooring.

      Cayenne pepper and white sage anti-clockwise

Southern fire, burn out her love at dawn
salamander her from his forges, let her
flame another gypsy's campfire
and sing of your fresh spark.

      Cayenne pepper and white sage anti-clockwise

Wind from the east, blow the scales
from her eyes, show his goat face, O
turn her tears to ice, crystal her in blue
till spring lets her breathe your sweet air.

      Cayenne pepper and white sage anti-clockwise

Crossed over

Your emails come as if from the other side
without preamble, enquiry, *politesse*
stark messages of residual business, or
re children's welfare.
Not requests, demands.
You've forgotten both my name and your own.

What is it that you want?

I want to ignore these electronic ghosts.
I don't believe you deserve an afterlife, but
you're still here apparently
knocking on the Ouija board
disturbing my repose. I'd better reply

Dear departed,

How to ward off the sky

have the crows scream at thunder
a caw is a caw is a caw, rolling

let the seagulls wheel before shelter
white flash, a squawk in the blue black

leave my burnt face at the window
fat rain, my tears lost, cooling

a cry is a cry is

bring wood pigeon calling dawn again
a coo, soothing

and the blackbird to chorus clean air
a trill is a trill is a thrill.

Woman waving

Three decades reduced in as many minutes

one

all the possible colours you can think of for fish
blue boxes, rainbow wrasse
anemone gardens jewelled in welcome
a clear deep sea, branching coral touches the sky

and the next

a tanker passes leaching its cargo
the reef breaks in its wake, white bones
feel no pain in tarry sand charnelled
with coke bottles, picnic plates, a plastic pool chair

the flotsam of life jettisoned as still-a-teenager
you said *I'm dumping you*
forgetting oil disperses with detergent
and I am an exceptionally strong swimmer

next—

Into this century

less than a thousand
days down
on just one beachhead
wind makes me rawboned
eye strung, sand blown
salt pierced.

Two-faced surfer boy
I recoil from your
wetsuit sexy wax caress
and swim unmarked
as fish in rocks
on Jurassic shores.

That's how I want to remember
our beginning
our soft shell of love
forget the savage.
Oh, let me gasp
once again, seemingly
beheaded, bitten, eaten.

My words drowning
St. George's Church, Madaba

No more than a clouded ditch   silt   silt
you could've crossed it in a couple of strokes
if not for the guards   halt   halt
hoisting their rifles, ready to unload them into you.

That's the thing about borders, temptation
here be dragons, ogres   fie   fie
you're off the edge of the map
and that's the thing about maps   lies   lies

one man's vision, as in the church floor
mosaicked with fish   flash   flash
there for the taking into teaming nets
the scale of them feeding thousands   five   six

reality is minnows or similar –
grey bodies between bright weed   slip   slip
on the day when we imagined immersion
but stuck to the rules and regs   tick   tick

– and they wouldn't feed the cat, without
let's call it a miracle.

And also his wife

On my knees in the August grass
sun blind, I clip your grave
where the council mower has missed.

I pull the dead blooms, add fresh,
wipe gull traces and set
the marble vase straight, or as near as.

Wait.

You're not here yet. Our dates
aren't on the slate. You're not beloved
husband with a half-blank stone
awaiting my name and a draped urn.

You've saved me an afternoon's work,
actually years of damp afternoons inflaming
my arthritis. Thanks for that.
No, really. Thanks for that.

Crimes of passion domestic violence repairing

I am not porcelain
      more earthenware mother
      the hard wearing stuff
      wheel-spun or moulded
      either way hand shaped

      you can cook with me
      or put me in the dishwasher
yet I break when dropped
as if I was

and that's why I long for gold
kintsugi   the art of repair.

You know, like buses

I

Dropping her bags, the girl backed herself against the Tube wall and banged her head, repeatedly and so hard, blood almost flowed into the memory of his words 'I do love you, but that's something for another time'. Tears soaked her face. Hysteria, or close.

'You look like you could do with a hug.' From the blur of her mascara she saw the outstretched arms of a young blonde woman. 'Thank you. I could.'

'So what exactly…' 'Men, or a man.' 'Ah. Is that all? Forget him. There'll be another along in a minute. You know, like buses.'

II

Back to square one – fresh start – new start – new beginning – tabula rasa – empty page – white space – blank canvas – blank slate – clean slate – clean sheet – vacancy – your name here – waiting for the next one to come along – you know – like buses.

III

The girl snarled, formed her left hand into a gun and held it up, black nail varnish facing outwards. 'Life's a killer,' she said before crossing her index and middle fingers and half-winking.

Her sense of humour wrong footed him, sometimes bang on, sometimes intently confusing, but he smiled and kissed her anyway. She started to relax for the first time that week. He could feel the tension leaving her body as she softened against his chest.

He liked this power, his ability to catch and check her and that she needed him for this. It made him feel safe. No danger he'd be replaced by anyone coming along in a minute, you know, like buses.

The messengers

not the scudding waves
not the wide bay
not the palms with new fronds
not the window or its frame
not the balcony
not the rocky promontory
not the beach
not the fishing boats
not the clouds as tall as sails
not the ivy
not the iron balustrade
but pigeons in their lofts
fat as eggs.

Stour story

The great white egret is windblown
on page one. Wings fanned
she's barely recognisable
flusters the hunt, goes hungry.

Next day same muddy shoreline
same bird, feathers smooth as hat silk
her catches easy, her belly full.

The whim of air and light
on water, as any tale
palpable in its writing.

February on the Regent's Canal

A chestnut flare away against the damp
and someone's firewood, the elegant wren
gives me a little of herself on this nothing day:
the sky low with cloud, no light rising, none
falling; an ivy on common tree trunks, muddy,
tripping on pavements, uneven, sprained afternoon.

But cheer is mushroom soup, smoked cheddar,
good bread, friends, and the wren
flicking her tail – a semaphore of welcome.

Oyster on the tideline

Not that I'm shy about my flesh
though I wish it less scarred and southern

there are few men who have seen
me naked. You join them now

for this intimacy. Private, away from
all, you tell me to disrobe.

Unblinking I obey. There's something
about the light on this shore

that makes it natural, like salt worn boards
or prized flint pebbles

but when I propose a streak from hut
to the sea, you explain the limits.

Civilisation and the neighbours
who'll, no doubt, be first in line

to see me posed on the blue sofa in oils.

Hooking a trout

Simple with the right kind of fly
blue curved May or tendrilled Caddis
well dressed, pinned in the case with art
ready for one bright morning
one quiet river.

      Mind your fingers
as you tie it to the line, don't
want to draw blood before you've loosed
those yards of thin flash and flicked them
onto the water. If you've judged
it takes minutes for the young one
to open his mouth and latch on.

Oh, you are good, all those years
of practice, reeling fast enough
to pull him across the surface
before he can go down for air.

Thought you'd have tired of this game, but
fresh flesh, a little mouth rip…
Toss him. He'll be back tomorrow.

The azul bay

When we stay in the stone house of rough-cast rooms
white-washed walls and slate floors

that you'll say should remind me of home
just without the grey, the morning sun will

purple the flags and release their sea memories.
I'll doze in those ancient waves, you'll wake me

with coffee, bread conjured warm
and that morning's eggs, a gentle benediction.

Later, I'll untease my hair by the crooked window
as you split logs for hearth and stove

knowing I'll have taken all the water. At night
we'll blanket up and wait for the switch of fireflies.

You'll take my hand and say something I won't catch.
You won't repeat it. The moment will be gone.

*

The slate flags are matt black out of the sun
that autumns through the crooked window

cutting the white room in two.
It's only a step to the lilac waves.

On days when the moment isn't gone
you lace our fingers and squeeze as if

we are about to go together. I'm afraid
to lose this hearth, these rough-washed walls

the you I do have. My throat pulses, urgent.
You never say. I'm left with a glance. Dare I?

*

Rumour brought me back, they say you shouldn't
old haunts, loves, too many ghosts.

The rough stone had lost its footing, the slates
shattered, the hearth stoved in by a roof beam,

the wood pile had shrunk, no-one needed it for winter
and the crooked window was unhinged.

I thought I saw you in its glass,
a one second glance. Without knowing

I cracked egg shells under my toes
from that spring's nesting.

I'd swear there was coffee brewing
though the water long disconnected.

Remembering you, Ronda

Once, a postcard, the picture curved
around the ring, a fight crowd
waiting for the start.

You wrote something loving
I forget now, but not too much
for the post or my parents.

I was grateful there was no actual
blood, it was all before,
there were smiles.

Asking after it, you pointed to
a face at the end of a row
said it was you.

Perhaps, perhaps not
I took your word, as always.

                    *

My finger down a red door
in the corrida, tracing
the gouge of a bull's horn.

You're here somewhere
in the empty stands, behind
photographs of jaded matadors

and visiting celebrities. Again
though, I'm glad there's no gore.

Woman taken by a wave

No matter the weather, it has to be said
you are persistent, lapping at my door
leaving me gifts, pebbles to rock my sleep
cowries to hold your song, though
I can do without the sideways scratch
of fractured crab legs and the stench of sea lice.

I like the way you always sigh
when you see me, that grand moan and, yes,
I love your white beard now, the promise
of spume stinging my face. I long for the day
you'll come with riches, sponges for my skin
coral and pearls for my throat.

Today you covered me and woke me
to the tropics. Come then, roll me in the surf.
Let's see where the current takes us.

How I'll wait for you

By pitch, my tanned thighs
tensed for your touch
velvet in the dark

by star in a silk slip
crushed and rippling
on the pink breeze

by streetlight as I
glow my lips
and nipples with gloss

by crescent moon, dressed
only in a bracelet
a snake with its silver tail

in its silver mouth
or, in nothing at all
save a splash of scent.

I am going to flirt with you outrageously every day

Take my hand
lead me to where you most want
my touch. Leave the rest to me.

I sweep almond oil over and deep
into your back
smell of lemongrass and ginger.

My fingertips circle your head
temple to nape
scent of lavender.

I turn the smart spring wind into
spearmint on your neck
brushing your skin.

I am coiled around you
glistening, silver
flicking my tongue on your ear.

Sing of my lips, bold on yours
soft to your lead, our tongues
twist and twin, dancing.

The press of my palms on your chest
my kiss on your heart
a black fig torn, devoured.

The sweep of my fresh washed hair
painting your ribs
its perfume filling you, breathe.

As I ground your ankles, show me
the flex and strength of your legs
your gentle power.

I stretch out your toes, they lengthen
in the early morning grass
cool on damp earth.

You are rested. I am at your
most wanted side
take my hand, lead.

Study of everything that changes in space and time

or geography, as defined, has me making
google maps, asking directions, tracing
flight lines, pinpointing your location
from every text and facebook post.

I dot and route you in blue
repeat, positioning myself in red.

Together we've made an imperial progress
Europe, Asia Minor
nine countries, six months, sometimes
just weeks apart

so rarely the same place or time zone
as if we're satellites orbiting.

When we do land there's no other
world, no work, duty, demands
all our bedrock is mudstone, and rivers
meander to a flat sea

where there's no such thing as long shore drift.

In a basket I bring you

oil for your body
lavender, rosemary
honey for your lips
the same

bass and bream
their eyes sparkling
the sun on the sea
the same

a gap in limestone
you can swim through
a cleft, a cave
the same

the juice of agaves
a pine tree
I'm Calypso
remember my name.

Metronome

I worry about you out there
in the chill of your life
where I am not.

I fret about time
its insistent beat
on your chest.

Never enough to work
let alone play
let alone love.

And that is all I ask
those minutes
for you to love me

quickly, softly,
quickly, hotly.

I live for one month
on a hour of you
but your heart

is pressed. I'm scared
your strength
will one day fade.

Everything: right place, time

In this climate
green figs drop
but never ripen
or rarely

only in those summers
when the sun
is constant
the walls
heat reflective

so don't pick them.

Come with me
somewhere warm
let's burst their seeds
in our greedy mouths
gorge till our breasts
and bellies ache

and we lie syrup soaked
sated, away
from this land
where figs are rare
and never ripe.

I've found the stopcock

Though it's been raining needles in this place for many months, longer, the season, longer, an age, longer, this epoch, and I've filled more buckets than there are under all the kitchen sinks in all the houses in this town, it is time.

That's me splayed, naked on a rumpled bed, sheets creased and slipping, quilt floored, my beads piled on the night stand, my head off the pillow. I'm tousle-haired, asleep, a little dead, smiling, contented.

You're at the window looking back at me, re-discovered woman, your once great love. Is it what you want?

Even though lights are on in the daytime and you're letting in cold air from the casement, no, more than cold, air piqued with frost, I can see your answer with my eyes closed.

I am oddly content

A partial health, but I won't bore you
with my ailments

shelter – calming, clean, private, mine
white walls make for peace

old friends and anyone who listens
with interest

a wardrobe that is more than coverings
clothes I can't wait to wear

food that nourishes, sustains, delights
seasonal treats which become staples –

oysters, truffles, asparagus
a happiness of small things

that make me stop and smile –
a dawn blackbird in the city, sugar

the sun on my skin, a kiss.

Acknowledgements

Earlier versions of these poems have appeared in:

And other poems ('Salomé in the mirror', Penelope: identity theft'), *Blackbox Manifold* ('The filthy quiet'), *Ink, Sweat & Tears* ('The proof of being able to cook'), *Lapidus*, ('February on the Regent's Canal'), *Poetry Ireland Review*, ('Everything: right place, time'), *Tears in the Fence* ('You know, like buses' and 'My words drowning'), *The High Window* ('The sun makes me'), *The Interpreter's House* ('Line-dancing at lunchtime'), *The Opiate* ('And also his wife'), *The Wolf* ('Crimes of passion domestic violence repairing'), *Under the Radar* ('Glass'), *Wedgie* ('Crimes of passion domestic violence, counting', 'Turning over, Daphne', 'Oyster on the tideline').

'Intifada, or the crow's carol' was anthologised by Eyewear Publications: *Refuges Welcome: Poems in a Time of Crisis*, 2015.

I thank their editors here.

Many thanks to all at Parthian, especially my patient and careful editor, Susie Wild.